GOODNIGHT GOES RIDING
And Other Poems

Copyright © Rod Miller, 2014

All rights reserved. No part of this book may be reproduced, scanned, or distributed in any printed or electronic form without express written permission.

Please do not participate in or encourage piracy of copyrighted materials in violation of the author's rights. Purchase only authorized editions.

Published and printed in the United States by Pen-L Publishing, Fayetteville, Arkansas www.Pen-L.com

ISBN: 978-1-940222-63-9
ebook: 978-1-940222-64-6

Cover design by Jay Griffith, Holmes & Co.
Formatting by Kelsey Rice

This book is dedicated to Earl Pickles, with whom the author has had the privilege of co-writing some fine cowboy poems.

Other Books by Writer Rod Miller:

Poetry:
Things a Cowboy Sees and Other Poems
Newe Dreams

Fiction:
Rawhide Robinson Rides the Range
Cold as the Clay
The Assassination of Governor Boggs
Gallows for a Gunman
Forthcoming: Rawhide Robinson Rides the Tabby Trail

Nonfiction:
Go West: The Risk and the Reward
Massacre at Bear River: First, Worst, Forgotten
John Muir: Magnificent Tramp
Forthcoming: The Lost Frontier: Momentous Moments
in the Old West You May Have Missed

VISIT WWW.WRITERRODMILLER.COM

GOODNIGHT GOES RIDING
And Other Poems

Rod Miller
Spur Award-winning poet and author

𝒫
Pen-L Publishing
Fayetteville, AR
Pen-L.com

CONTENTS

Foreword..ix

Author's Note...xvii

Introduction..xix

ONE: The Wild West
Goodnight Goes Riding...1
Migrations..3
Tools of the Trade..4
Equitation Equation 6
Boot Salute..7
Don't Just Sit There..9
Lamentation for a Living Legend...............................11
Don't Ask Me..13
Heads or Tails 14
Nothing Extra..16
A Good Hand With A Rope.....................................17
Song of the Stampede..19
The Hunt for Rafael Lopez.....................................21
Aftershock..23
One old cowboy's lunchsack opinions.......................24
Not Counting Saddlebags 25
Mule Whisperer 28
Riding Old Red..29
Square Peg...30
Spring Works Sonnet..32

TWO: Arena Dirt
What Goes Cowboy Up...35
The Colorful Pageantry of Rodeo............................36
Rodeo Coming! 38

Before the Dance..40
Lending a Hand a Hand..41
Barrel Roll 43
Crowd Pleaser...44
Preliminary Aftermath...45
Second Opinion 46
For Love...47
On the Road...49
Acquired Taste...50
Tied for the Average 52
Horses of a Different Color......................................54
Gear Bag..56

THREE: Ruminations
Haiku for a Cowboy's Education..............................61
Long Time Ago 62
The Travail, Which God Hath Given.........................64
The Second Book of Job 66
Manifest Destiny..68
Upon Stony Places...69
Haiku for Autumn 70
Keeping the Books...71
Semi-Retired 72
Haiku for a Horseback Morning................................74
Gone 75
Haiku for Hunger..76
Packsaddle...77
The Beauty of Mountains...78

Acknowledgements...81

About the Author..83

FOREWORD
by A.J. Mangum

Rod Miller first crossed my radar when I became the editor of *Western Horseman* magazine, for which Rod had been a frequent contributor, authoring poems and feature articles on rodeo athletes, musicians, artists and frontier history. In the genre of contemporary western non-fiction, in which the talent pool can be frighteningly shallow, Rod stood out from the crowd as a bona fide journalist and poet, one truly inspired by his subjects, and in possession of the writing chops to tell their stories with honesty, clarity and respect.

In his features and profiles, Rod steers clear of the Marlboro Man mythology that weighs down, even negates, so much of what's presented as journalism about the contemporary West. Instead, he strives to produce lively, meaningful documentation of a culture for which he happens to possess a deep passion. With a reporter's eye, he sees through affectations and clichés, and chases subjects that share a certain rawness, a collective identity shaped by a sense of adventure and a reverence for horses and the natural world. Rod's non-fiction is, at its heart, a modern twist on the real-life saga of the untamed frontier.

Likewise, Rod's poetry is infused with a genuineness that elevates his work above the medium's predictable yarns and gives the reader a front-row seat at a captivating reality-based dramedy. You observe from a respectful distance the poignant moment shared by a young girl and her horse. You take a seat at the kitchen table in a ranch house in which the "romance of cowboy life" is balanced against the realities of mortgages, droughts and volatile markets. And you're let in on the West's unique brand of humor, shaped by hard luck, eccentricity, and the unpredictability of lives shaped by the land, weather and livestock. Rod is a truthteller.

And truth can, on occasion, be dangerous.

There's an anecdote I've never shared with Rod (until now). One morning, more than a decade ago, while I was still with *Western Horseman*, my phone rang, interrupting a hurried round of last-minute proofreading. The first words from the caller: "I got a complaint about an article y'all ran." The caller directed me to a specific page in that year's February issue.

I'm sure I sighed heavily and rolled my eyes as I pushed aside a stack of as-yet-unproofed article layouts, pulled the issue in question from my bookshelf, and navigated to the page number the caller had referenced, at which point I likely rolled my eyes yet again.

The caller had used the word "article." I was sure he wanted to vehemently disagree with the horsemanship regimen prescribed in an instructional piece, or share some seedy gossip about the subject of a recent personality profile. The page in question, though, didn't contain a section of an "article." It was home to one of Rod's poems, a work that contains what is perhaps my favorite Rod Miller storyline.

In the poem, a rancher complains about a hired hand who takes a frustratingly casual approach to his work. The hand is increasingly unreliable; his work goes undone as he wastes the day with catnaps and childish games; he's incapable of putting work ahead of play, leaving the rancher, who's narrating the story, with few options. At the end of the poem, said rancher expresses great regret at having to fire the hand, who is revealed in the poem's final syllable to be the rancher's father.

Despite my dry recap above, the poem is a hilarious, yet profound, commentary on the passing of a ranch from one generation to the next. In my reading (and subsequent overthinking), the son has likely observed his father's role closely and aspired to it for as long as he can recall, but even as he assumes leadership of the family business, has little appreciation for the toll the job will take, or the relief his father must feel in handing over the reins to the outfit.

To continue my over-analysis: The father, after a lifetime of hard labor, has resolved to seize every opportunity to enjoy each moment of his remaining years. In his behavior, which so confuses his son, there's an unbridled joy that brings to mind the antics of many aging cowboys who've been lucky enough to trade the burdens of their work for a brand of overdue wild abandonment. Both the son's consternation and the father's casual lack of concern – over anything – bring smiles to my face, as well as memories of my father and my uncles, any of whom I can picture in the role of the father in Rod's poem.

DEALING WITH PHONE CALLS from confused readers is one of the less appealing line items in a magazine editor's job description, as you're often put in the awkward position of having to tactfully inform a stranger that he might be an idiot. When I landed on Rod's poem, I figured the caller had simply referenced the wrong issue.

"Sir, are you sure you're talking about the February issue?" I (probably) asked. "Because the February issue actually came out in January, so you might be thinking of ...."

"No, it's the February issue. I'm looking at it right here."

"Do you have the right page number? Because I'm looking at that page, and it's actually not an article. It's a poem by Rod Miller, and ...."

"That's the one. That's the article I'm talking about."

What followed was simply bizarre.

The caller had taken Rod's clearly fictional poem (written in rhyming verse and illustrated by a cartoon) to be a non-fiction, journalistic report about a ranch on which a senior citizen had been unjustly fired. The caller insisted that the rancher should be ashamed of himself, and demanded both the rancher's name and an apology by the magazine for its unfair reporting of the situation, which seemed to the caller entirely too one-sided. No one had even interviewed the old man.

I swear I am not making this up.

In the background of the call, I could hear excited, angry chatter. The caller wasn't alone. I pictured a kitchen full of people (who somehow had nothing better to do at 10 in the morning) riled up at the treatment of a character in a poem one of them had stumbled across in a magazine that happened to be on the table. They were so upset, they were interrupting one another with imagined observations about the offending "article."

"How could an employer be so...?!?"

"It's age discrimination! It's...!"

"Such a lack of respect for his own...!"

"And it's the older generation that taught us to...!"

I was confident I wasn't the victim of a practical joke. The call was real. At an appropriate gap in the din emanating from the other end of the line, I began improvising for the caller a simplistic explanation for the words (and the cartoon!) that appeared on the page before him.

"Sir," I (probably) began. "This is a poem. You may have noticed it's written in stanzas and the lines rhyme, which isn't a traditional format for the reporting of a news story. This isn't something that actually happened."

I think I then began some misguided attempt at literary analysis: generational perspectives, themes derived from the pressures of ranching economics, potential backstories of the key characters – all for nought. I think I lost the guy at "This is a poem."

The call did not end well. By that point, I'd been a magazine editor for a dozen years and had endured hours of unearned abuse from uninformed strangers with an abundance of free time. Whereas I might've once allowed even the craziest of callers to believe he'd successfully made his point, for no other reason than to end a call and get back to work, I'd reached a stage at which I was perfectly happy to let a deranged crank bellow into the void as I (at best) half-listened, registering only that he was still consuming oxygen, as I perused paperwork or browsed headlines on the Internet.

When this particular caller realized I wasn't giving in – that I would not agree to a printed apology, or even agree to characterize the poem in question as a news story steeped in controversy – there was some parting shot about sabotaging newsstand sales in his corner of Oklahoma.

More power to you, I thought, confident neither the caller nor his entourage could possibly have the wherewithal to locate a bookstore or newsstand. Somewhere in the Sooner State's Osage County, there is a *Western Horseman* subscriber still fuming, his ire unrequited.

The poem in question follows this Foreword.

AS FOR MY POINT: Rod Miller's work – even his fiction, obviously even his poetry – is steeped in reality. His explanations of a character's motivations, his descriptions of an environment or a set of sensory experiences or the play-by-play of an action-sequence ... even when they're pure fiction, even when they're riotously funny, there's a vital realism that infuses his work with unquestionable credibility, so much so that, at least for certain categories of readers, the simplest of yarns can be mistaken for hard-hitting news reports. Despite such dangers, that ever-present foundation of truth allows Rod to get past the surface novelty of a subject and offer readers greater meaning – greater understanding – through vicarious experiences and unexplored viewpoints. It's an end goal to which every writer should aspire.

A.J. Mangum is the editor of Ranch & Reata *magazine.*

No Enjoyment in Unemployment

His staples won't stick to fence posts,
Nor his brands to a slick calf's hide.
And I'm weary of hearing his lying boasts
About the rank broncs he can ride.

He never remembers to pack a lunch
And he's forever bummin' a smoke;
His turn to buy a round for the bunch
Somehow always finds him broke.

His loops won't fit over a critter's head,
Nor can they find their way to a hock.
He often gets lost right here on the spread
When sent out to gather stock.

The calves he castrates get infection.
The hay he bales turns to mold.
Colts he schools all need correction
If we hope to get them sold.

His saddle horses are cinch-galled
With sore backs and withers fistulous.
His lasso rope is so twisted and balled
And kinked and knotted it's ridiculous.

His tack is always in disrepair.
Horseshoes he nails on never fit.
Compare his saddle to his easy chair
And you'll see where he'd rather sit.

The chaps he borrowed have gone astray.
The spurs I loaned him are missing too.
And I have to follow him around every day
To do the jobs he forgets to do.

I guess you can see why I let him go;
He's the sorriest hand I've ever had.
But, still, I just can't help feeling low
About giving the sack to my Dad.

AUTHOR'S NOTE

This collection features poems about the American West. Some conform, more or less, to the styles of rhyme and meter typical of cowboy poetry. Others wander off that trail to include poems with rhyme but no meter and poems with neither rhyme nor meter. Some of my friends in the cowboy poetry universe will find the latter troubling, and a few will dismiss such poems altogether, refusing to even acknowledge free verse as poetry.

But, cowboys routinely break out of the pen and jump fences and shed hobbles and otherwise escape fetters in many aspects of life and, to me, that spirit also applies to poetry. Besides, as my friend DW Groethe puts it, "I don't waste my time on the debate. I have better things to do."

As for the introductory poem, "An Apology to Readers, Sort Of, But More Like an Explanation or Maybe an Excuse," I mean every word of it. Please forgive my poetic inadequacies and cut me some slack.

INTRODUCTION

*An Apology to Readers, Sort Of,
But More Like an Explanation
or Maybe an Excuse*

I don't like poems about writing poems
And the way a verse comes to be;
How I write and erase, rewrite and rephrase
Doesn't matter to anyone but me.

But lately I've gotten more sensitive
To stings from readers' complaints
About imperfect rhymes some of the time,
And syntax that should be better, but ain't.

Or about metaphors whittled square
That don't fit into analogies round;
Or feet that bumble and meters that stumble
And stagger with an offbeat sound.

Writing poems, though, ain't as easy
As it looks from up there on the fence.
When you assemble words from an unruly herd
The results don't always make sense.

The alphabet, you see, is a rough string
That don't take kindly to being broke.
You corral 'em and then they run around your pen
Stirring up dust that'll blind and choke.

Wrangling words ain't no Sunday picnic
And I don't know what readers expect—
With 26 letters all fighting their fetters
It stands to reason there'll be a few wrecks.

ONE
The Wild West

ONE
The Wild West

Goodnight Goes Riding

He rides and he rides
Across so plain an expanse
That an anthill is an eminence
And a buffalo wallow a landmark.
And he rides.

Shortgrass stems nod in
Insistent wind, waving
Through more miles than he sees
As he nods in the saddle
As he rides.

As he rides,
The saddle stops rocking
And his eyes open to see
A maw in the Llano
Fall away from the forefeet
Of the horse he rides.

Raven wings silently
Slice the sky below.
Juniper green gashes
Its way down the canyons to
Sip at Prairie Dog Town Fork.
And he rides.

He rides a game trail
Off the caprock,
Wends past hoodoos of
Eroded Permian
Imagining longhorns
Grazing under shaded
Mesas and mesquite.

Plants a ridgepole over a
Badger hole, nails up a door
And calls Palo Duro home
For himself and
A hundred thousand cattle.

And he rides.
He rides.

Migrations

I hear them in the evening winging northward—
    Their eager, maybe longing, kind of sound.
It reminds me that we'll soon be done with calving;
    That branding time ain't far from coming 'round.

And I think how fall works really ain't that distant;
    Shipping calves under sundown pewter skies
Wherein arrowpointed flocks are winging southward,
    Trailing echoes of urgent, mournful cries.

Tools of the Trade

Three busted legs on the left side and another one on
    the right.
Feet both mashed when falling broncs chose them as places
    to light.
Near lost an eye to a broken rope. Dallies took a finger and
    a half.
Got twisted in the coils and 'bout lost an arm one time
    roping a calf.

        For forty years I forked a horse
        for forty a month and found;
        two score years in the stirrups
        at forty a month and found.

Pile-driving mounts on cold mornings rattled my
    backbone loose,
leaping and lunging and plunging, snapping my neck like
    a noose.
Black nails on a thumb and two fingers. Horseshoe nail
    scars on the rest.
Hoof tracks all up and down both legs. Bite marks all
    over my chest.

        For forty years I forked a horse
        for forty a month and found;

>   two score years in the stirrups
>   at forty a month and found.

Plumbing runs slow, if at all, from leather pounding
    my backside.
Knees so bowed a dog can run through. Toes point
    outward and wide.
My hips are kinked in a permanent bend, fingers curled to
    fit reins.
There's no part of me that ain't used up—if you don't
    count my brains.

>   For forty years I forked a horse
>   for forty a month and found;
>   two score years in the stirrups
>   at forty a month and found.

From winters up on the high line to summers down on
    the border,
all those outfits over all those years couldn't have
    worked me harder.
They took all I had—and not just me—used every hand
    they could find.
But with all they took—and all they used—they never
    wanted my mind.

>   For forty years I forked a horse
>   for forty a month and found;
>   two score years in the stirrups
>   at forty a month and found.

Equitation Equation

The laws of nature are immutable;
Mathematical laws are inscrutable;
Now and then with these realities I collide:
That equations must balance
In each and every circumstance
Is at odds with what happens when I ride.

Each time I saddle up and mount,
By a strict mathematical count,
One dismount is required for equilibrium.
But my equestrian situation
Disagrees with that calculation—
I fall off horses more often than I get on 'em.

Boot Salute

Boots. Boots with runover heels
Dangling spur rowels like tiny wheels.
Some cracked, split, with leaking holes
And only memories of soles.

Branding pen boots splashed with blood.
Windmill boots layered with mud.
Rubber boots to water hay.
Galoshes for a winter day.

Worn and dull, scratched and scuffed.
Sunday boots, shiny and buffed.
Dancing boots, likely to kick.
Barhopping boots, smeared with sick.

Boots piled up by the back door,
In the car's trunk, on the truck floor.
Young. Old. Boots of all ages—
Tally books; calendar pages.

Most joined up like man and wife.
A few doomed to an orphan's life.
Now and then they get mismatched
When in the dark a "pair" gets snatched.

But I've got boots, thanks be to God;
If not for boots, I'd go unshod.
Don't know how to tie shoelaces.
Boots. All the time, all places.

Don't Just Sit There

It's held a gather of henhouse eggs
and huckleberries plucked in the wild.
It's fanned a passel of recalcitrant mounts
bucking out ornery and riled.

I wave it around whilst sorting calves
—I'll even throw it to turn one back—
and it's mighty handy as a bludgeon
to beat off a mad cow attack.

It affectionately swats my wife's backside,
and balky horses, smart on the rump.
It's been feed bucket for a bait of grain
and trough for water drawn from a pump.

It's even been used as a signal flag
to start a Fourth of July race.
And it's done lots of duty at naptime
as a sunshade plopped over my face.

It sweeps snow from saddle seat in winter
and brushes summer dust off my duds.
(It once served as emergency underwear
when I's caught unaware in the bathtub.)

It's no wonder it's worn out and weary,
battered and tattered till it looks half dead
—I've kept this old hat so damn busy
it ain't had time to just sit on my head.

Lamentation for a Living Legend

You're cold and wet all winter.
In summer, hot and dry.
You're all of the above in spring and fall;
It's always freeze or fry.

And the wind is your constant companion,
Blowing all the year round;
Chilled by icebergs or hot from hell's oven
It tumbles over the ground.

The weeds and the trees and the bushes
Are thorny, spiny, and sharp.
Every stone and boulder for miles around
Collects 'neath your bedroll tarp.

The food is monotonous and awful
And tends to stick in the craw;
It's always served up the same shade of brown
And what ain't overcooked is raw.

The horses all buck every morning
And sull up in the afternoon,
They spook when you get close to cattle;
Come apart when it's least opportune.

The cows are panicky and skittish;
They run at the drop of a hat;
And always stampede in the badlands and
Breaks; never out on the flat.

You work every day and part of each night
For wages pitifully small.
All you own is a kack and your sougans
And whatever your saddlebags haul.

Yet the books make us out to be heroes.
About us, epics are made
That say working cattle a-horseback
Is a life we would not trade.

This work, steeped in myth and legend,
Could make a feller a snob—
If it weren't for the fact that we're cowboys
'Cause we can't find a decent job.

Don't Ask Me

I know it ain't The Cowboy Way
And that's why I'm ashamed to say
That this cowboy cannot dance.
I used to try, when I got the chance,
To two-step, waltz, and swing.
But dancing—it just ain't my thing.
I could dance when I used to drink.
At least that's what I used to think.
I thought that I was handsome, too,
But stone cold sober, neither was true.
So I quit tripping the light fantastic
When I realized my moves were spastic.
And there's another reason I'd rather sit
When it comes to dancing; why I quit:
Whether dancing to jukeboxes or live bands,
Other dancers kept stepping on my hands.

Heads or Tails

"It seems to me," the old man says
Whilst carving away on a stick,
"That with all your years of schoolin'
You've yet to learn a lick."

I'm clinching nails on his old blue mare
In the heat of a midsummer's day;
Three more mounts in line for footwear
—Shoein's how I earn my pay.

The old feller spits and whittles
And passes judgment now and then
From his seat on an upturned bucket
In the skimpy shade of the hog pen.

"You're a mite unsteady with that rasp,"
He says, "that shoe ain't sittin' quite flat."
He did it better in his day, he says,
And without no diploma, at that.

"I never had much eddication," he says,
"Shod horses 'cause it's all I knew."
Spits and whittles, says, "Watch that quick!"
And, "Don't be shapin' the hoof to the shoe!"

Then, "Looks to me like a feller like you,
What with college and the books he's read,
Oughta be smart enough for a better job—
One where his butt ain't higher'n his head."

For Marc Otte

Nothing Extra

There's Red and Rusty, Buster and Buck
And Jesse and Jake and Cody and Chuck;
There's Slim and there's Pete, Logan and Ty,
And J-W, J-R, T-C, and P-Y.

But *Joseph Ernest Nephtali Dufault*?
Does that sound like any cowboy you know?
No ranny, no twister, no peeler or waddy
Would sport a name so pretentious and gaudy.

Nor does a handle like that attached to a Canuck
Paint a picture of a man who could ride horses that buck.
But this drifter knew broncs; was, in fact, a top hand
Who topped off remudas across this wide land,

Became rich and famous, known far and wide
As an hombre with caballos, a man who could ride.
So it's best not to put too much stock in names—
This *Dufault* you don't know, you know as *Will James*.

A Good Hand With A Rope

I seen him do it a hundred times:
give lie to the idea that a cowboy
won't do no job
that can't be done horseback.

Many's the day he'd ride in
from his cow work, strip his saddle,
shoo his horse into the corral,
and untie his forty-foot hemp.

For a score and fourteen years
he'd cowboyed that country,
making a hand for any brand he wanted
then for good reason or none at all

draw his time and try other pastures
when it suited him.
He seemed content, then, alone in the
bunkhouse of our one-hired-hand outfit.

Those late days I'd finish up
the barnyard chores—splashing a pail
of water into the henhouse trough,
milking half the cow and giving the

hind tits to her penned-up calf and an
adopted dogie. He paid me attention
even though I's just a kid. Worse,
the boss's kid. Worse still, a girl.

He'd shake out a loop and snake a catch
on the gatepost and wrap the rope
around his hind end and sit on it till
it took a good bite. Then turn, turn, turn;

Counting cadence with skiprope rhymes
dredged up from a childhood no one knew
while I jump jump jumped in whipped-up
dust as amber air faded gray.

Song of the Stampede

On the far horizon, clouds pulse with lightning glow;
    Rolling thunder knots the night guard all up tight.
The cattle on their bellies chew cud and moan and low,
    But, in a flash, could rise in fear and flight.

Song seems insufficient, but he croons his repertoire
    Hoping against hope the melodies calm the storm.
The sky grows thick and heavy, twinkling nary a star,
    And grass leans into wind, gusty and warm.

Cocinero has a feeling, so the pots and pans get stowed
    And he rousts out the flunky, rolled in bed.
They wrestle with the wagon sheets to cover up the load
    As the wind tears clouds to tatters overhead.

The remuda paws and snorts; the nighthawk herds 'em close
    While night horse saddle cinches pull up snug.
The air is fairly crackling and the rain scent fills your nose
    Then boots fill empty stirrups like a plug.

With one eye on the cattle and the other to'ard the camp
    The night guard hopes that help is coming soon.
Lightning flashes close, steams and sizzles through the damp.
    Thunder swallows all that's left of his last tune.

Before the rumble fades away thunder of another kind
    Trembles the earth as cattle break and run.
Saddle horses race the torrent for any hoofhold they can find
    For if you stumble in the dark you are done.

Sun rises, come the morning, in a sky empty and blue.
    Scattered cattle graze as if there's nothing wrong.
Horses, heads hung low, carry the weary cowboy crew
    Nodding off to the meadowlark's daybreak song.

The Hunt for Rafael Lopez

Last seen, we suppose,
in the belly of the mountain
in darkness only Jonah knows.
The Minnie's drifts and stopes
concealing all—except the brilliance
of blood shed on mountain slopes,

crying out from lake shore,
spilled on streets,
the life drained from four.
His manna a pilfered lunchbox;
mean meals of immigrants
seeking a home among rocks.

The blackness of his lair
dimmed by smoke
sent by the law to find him there.
But he, a wisp, hovering at the Incline,
left in darkness another two
bleeding and dying.

Did it end in that mine, his luck?
His bones, in a powder
blast turned to muck
and hauled out mingled with ore,

stamped to dust in the mill
and swept from the floor,

the final judgment of Rafael
the refiner's fire—
the smelting and burning of hell;
a life, in the end, a total loss,
his epitaph:
Rafael Lopez: Dross.

Aftershock

Then, leaving a bloody
young Lot Huntington
splayed on the fence rails,
Rockwell rides away.

Doc Faust and them
of the posse who
saw the gunplay
stand stock still in the
drift of powder smoke in the
chill winter dawn.

Damn, some one of them
says. Fool kid ought to've
knowed better than to
draw down on ol' Port.

Then pistols spill out the
stage station door followed
by other horse thieves,
hands raised to heaven
or Rockwell
had he stayed to see it.

One old cowboy's lunchsack opinions offered in a young boy's presence one October afternoon on the Allotment

damn shore things's changed
be foolish to say other
but them goodoldays never
was same's they was—
gimme nother'n them readymades
—even back then

man namea Glidden
they say was what
laid the West to rest—
him with his coils uv
cherubim's swords straightenin
up all the edges uv the range—

but ain't no four strands uv
bobwar stapled to no cedar posts
long enough er strong enough
er wide enough er high enough
to fence in the cowboy
ner out neither one

Not Counting Saddlebags

"A woman's purse," the cowboy said,
"is a curious thing I don't get.
I've seen ladies tote them all my life
and I don't understand them yet.

"It seems a lot more stuff goes in
than ever comes back out—
always rubbish that no one needs;
just junk you could do without.

"You'll never see a cowboy tied
to something as silly as a reticule.
No ma'am, it'd never happen.
No man would be such a fool.

"A hand just wouldn't burden himself
with all that debris and mess
so he doesn't need some silly satchel
to pack it around," he says.

"That sounds to me," his wife replied,
"like what lands behind a bull.
You not only carry more containers,
you keep loading 'til they're all full.

"Start with those pockets on your vest.
One's bulging with a can of snuff.
The other's packed with horseshoe
nails, fence staples, and other such stuff.

"And both the pockets on your shirt
are stuffed with so much crap
like tally books and feed store receipts
that you can't even snap the flaps.

"Five more pockets on your pants.
And they still won't hold all your trash.
Pickup keys. Pocket knife. Pliers.
Empty checkbook. Fifty-two cents cash.

"Not to mention a pair of gloves,
whang leather, and pocket lint,
a set of rattlesnake rattles
and an arrowhead made of flint.

"And you've got the guts—or lack
of brains—to question a lady's purse?
These handbags may not be perfect,
but your method of packing is worse.

"The way you poke and prod for misplaced
bits is so indecent it's a scandal.
Women have the sense to consolidate
things, and to carry them with a handle.

"We never lose or mislay our things.
We can search every cranny and nook
and cubbyhole within seconds,
because there's only one place to look.

"So you see, you stupid cowboy,
a woman's handbag isn't funny.
If your way of doing things was half as
smart, maybe you'd get to carry the money."

Mule Whisperer

Horses by scores and dozens I've had between my heels,
And driven hitched to implements dragged or rolled
    on wheels.
Horses I've worked aplenty, but I've never handled a mule;
For they're obstinate and intractable and don't play by
    the rules.

Hybrids take special handling according to what I've seen—
Oversize lungs, an earsplitting voice, and a vocabulary mean,
Belching clouds of loud profanity that drift in a toxic mist;
Words that don't belong in any mouth a mother's kissed.

Like [EXPLETIVE], [DELETED], [CENSORED], and [BLEEP],
Calling mules [ASTERISKS], dumb as [CROSSED OUT] sheep;
[DELETED] and [BLEEP] and dirty [OBSCENITY] [CUT],
Threaten them with [STRIKE THROUGH]; no ifs, ands, or buts.

Muleskinners don't apologize for their filthy, nasty words—
Claim that what they're saying ain't the worst a mule
    has heard
And burning their big [BLEEPING] ears to gain the
    upper hand
Is the only kind of language them [EXPLETIVE]
    mules understand.

Riding Old Red

Old Red can travel the whole day long
From dawn until the gloaming.
And when I dismount for ground work
I never worry about her roaming.
She sits tranquil, doesn't stray or wander,
Rests quietly all the while—
Knowing I'll mount up once again,
And demand of her mile upon mile.

She flies quick and true across flat land.
Bears down to climb the hills.
Dodges trees and rocks and bushes.
Splashes through the rills.
She cares not about ire nor affection,
Ignores caress as well as shout;
As even tempered as an unfeeling machine,
She'll never sulk or pout.

Old Red asks little in exchange for work,
Her demands are few and fair:
Oil and gas to keep her running smooth
And the occasional shot of air.
She's the modern rancher's mount of choice,
This courser between my knees—
Old Red's not an old-fashioned horse you see;
She's one of them newfangled ATVs.

Square Peg

She saddled up when C.J. passed
And seldom after knew any other seat;
Ramrodded the men, bossed the cows,
Took over that ranch slick and neat.

Learned to sit a saddle smooth and easy,
Like a spot on a paint horse's back;
To ride all day, scrape a hip hole at night,
And eat from an old greasy sack.

Had a natural eye for horseflesh;
Found cow sense, somewhere, to spare.
Savvied herding and cutting and roping,
Cowboyed more than her share.

Tightened up fences around the place,
Kept thick carpets covering the ground,
Drifting the herd always toward better grass,
Watching the calves pile on pounds.

Started flooding meadows in springtime
To mow them down come late July,
Feeding fat herds there all winter long
from haystacks tight and high.

Old C.J.'s ranch was a flower, it seems,
That blossomed only after he died;
The place became such a showpiece
His dry bones likely swelled with pride.

So folks were surprised when she sold out
To take a place in the town one day.
"Running a ranch just isn't my pattern.
I'm cut out to keep house, and crochet."

A rocking chair on a cool screen porch
Was all she rode evermore,
Trading the monotonous creak of leather
For the squeak of a board in the floor.

Spring Works Sonnet

Scrub oak tangles on the slopes; only
spots and specks of sunshine sneak in
where the calf lies silent and lonely.
Breaking branches become a buckskin

horse with limb-fending cowboy aboard.
Whistles and shouts, instinct and insecurity
bring the calf to its feet, drive it toward
the branding fire, burning hair and blistery

hide. Bawling calves mother up, sucking
away the taste of smoke. Sated, they drift
from dusty chaos with the drive, bucking
and running upslope to oak leaves that sift

golden shadows from low sun at end of day
as the dun horse carries the cowboy away.

TWO
Arena Dirt

What Goes Cowboy Up...

"Cowboy up," says Marlowe,
"Don't give this horse an inch.
He'll swap ends and then suck back,"
he advises as he hooks my cinch.

"Cowboy up," says Shadow
as he pulls my latigo.
"Kick the hair off this old bronc
and you can win the go."

"Cowboy up," says Blizzard,
"You can ride Brownie to the bank
—if you can ride him at all," he grins
as he waits to yank the flank.

"Cowboy up," I tell myself
as I nod for Buster Brown.
He launches me in three and it's
cowboy up—and then it's cowboy down.

The Colorful Pageantry Of Rodeo

Soaring, diving wind-blown kites.
A dance of color under arena lights
On kaleidoscopic summer nights.

Red and blue and purple and green—
The prettiest flying colors you've seen.

Color blends, mixes and clashes.
Glowing orange like fire flashes.
Greens appear in smears and splashes.

Blue and purple, red and gold—
Colors fly by in flashes bold.

Flying divots of dirty dun mud.
Reds in all the hues of blood.
Streams of blue in roiling flood.

Green and blue and gold and white—
Brilliant colors, all in flight.

The sparkle of shiny chrome-plated steel
As conchos and snaps and buckles reel;
A silver spur on a boot's high heel.

Blue and purple; green and red—
Colors fly with wings widespread.

Cream-colored Guatemalan straw.
Whitened knuckles on a grasping claw.
The syrup-brown trail of dislodged chaw.

Spreading, swelling black and blue—
As colors smashed and crashed and flew.

The brilliant hues of a cowboy show?
The colorful pageantry of rodeo?
The answer, unfortunately, is no.

I bucked off bad, I'm sad to announce—
And it's only me as I roll and bounce.

Rodeo Coming!

The semi's stacks growl
as it slows to turn up the street.
Here they come, one says,
launching a stampede of feet

in scuffed up, worn out boots.
Hands hold down hats too big
as they shove and stumble
on the run to the arena. The rig

sits as if waiting, ticking and
tocking like a clock winding
down as they hit the fence at
speed, scrambling, climbing,

until elbows latch onto the
top rail and toes catch wire.
Breathless, wide-eyed, they
watch darkness climb higher

as the end gate rises, step
by squeaky step. *Here they
come*, he says again, as a
seventeen-hand barefoot bay

one-hops down the ramp.
Head high, nostrils wide
he snorts, once, twice, in
their direction. *I could ride*

that one, one boy bets.
Could not. Could too.
Could not. Well, maybe not—
but I could out-ride you.

Before the Dance

Spurred heel on the barre, nose to knee, they stretch and
    flex and extend,
muscle and tendon and joints warm up as they twist and
    turn and bend,
they reach and point an arabesque, strike attitude with
    bended knee:
the performers prepare out of sight, where audience
    does not see.
They spin around in a pirouette, feet fly in a fouetté
they leap and rise and float and glide in entrechat and jeté,
all to prepare for the main event, the partnering up,
    the pas de deux.
Their partners, in the meantime, mill aimlessly
    behind the chutes—
unconcerned, uncaring, these confederates
    who are not allies
twitch their tails and wiggle their hides to ward off
    pesky flies.

Lending a Hand a Hand

"I can do it," she says,
And it's sure enough true.
I'm just glad she doesn't add
The "better than you."

She can load and unload
Her horse and her tack
And handle that trailer
Driving forward or back.

She tosses around baled hay
And big sacks of grain,
Hauls buckets of water
Without stress or strain.

I just want to help, but
She don't need me for much—
To her, I'm as useless
As a foam-rubber crutch.

It's a sad state of affairs
For an old bronc rider like me
'Cause I'm sweet on this
Young barrel racer, you see,

And it's hard to make points
Or win her affection
When my every foray
Is met with rejection.

But what shatters my ego,
What hurts even more,
Is that compared to her
I'm a gunsel for sure;

Forget my regalia
And my bow-legged strut—
When it comes to cow*boy*ing,
That girl kicks my butt.

Barrel Roll

Two rights and a left
Or two lefts and a right,

You run 14 seconds
Then trailer all night.

A flying lead change.
Claw out of the turn.

Gather your legs and
Fly home on the burn

Breaking the beam as
You cross the mark.

The arena's glare
Fades into the dark

And it's down the road
To the next cloverleaf.

The runway is long.
The flight is brief.

Crowd Pleaser

Being a cowboy hero has
   Always been one of my plans—
      To perform in the rodeo arena
         For thousands of cheering fans.

      But choosing an event isn't easy—
    Each one is fraught with perils.
  But my dream came true, and now I drive
The truck that picks up the barrels.

Preliminary Aftermath

I pull my head out from under the dirt
And take a look around to see if I'm hurt.
The straps and buckles are gone from my chaps.
All that's left of my shirt is three pearl snaps.
My left boot is hither, the right one is yon.
My nose is flat and my eyebrows are gone.
Both of my ears cut nine-iron-size divots.
Nothing left of my pants but a few rags and rivets.
There are only two teeth still inside my mouth;
The others are spread to the east and the south.
My kneecaps have migrated up to my thighs.
The lids now cover the backs of my eyes.
My elbows and ankles have come unhinged.
What's left of my hair is ragged and fringed.
My ribs are all mushy, my fingers are bent.
It's a mystery to me where my underwear went.
I knew rodeo could get rough now and then—
But I'll never, ever, ride in the Grand Entry again.

Second Opinion

He was hung up and drug all around in the dirt
Stomped kicked and trampled and otherwise hurt.
He was knocked on the head and all in a daze,
So they called in the meat wagon and hauled him away.

The doc at the hospital gave him one glance
And said "Cut off those boots and that shirt and those pants.
We'd best get to work and get this guy mended,
If we don't there's a chance that his life will be ended!"

So they started in snipping and cutting away clothes
When the cowboy rose up and said *Get rid of those
Scissors! Hold on just a minute! You leave my duds alone!
Hold your horses!* he hollered, and *Wait! Hold the phone!*

"But mister, you don't understand," said the nurse,
"You may lose your clothes but the alternative's worse."
Well, to YOU, he said, *it may be just torn cloth and leather;
But just now it's the only thing holding ME together.*

For Love

You know going in you're
getting in line for some pain.
You've been hurt before.
Still, hopeful, you try again.

What is it they always say—
It'll get better with time?
Maybe. But that, too,
could be part of the lying.

There are even those who say
it won't hurt you to suffer.
Makes you stronger. Getting
over it makes you tougher.

Never mind. This time, you
know, won't be the same.
Sweat breaks. Eyes lock.
Hearts take aim.

You'll try again because it's
the only time you feel alive—
this eight-second affair
You know you'll survive,

but may lose. Because you know,
at this game, only one can win.
Still, pairing up with a bronc,
at least you know going in.

On the Road

Magpie on hot black asphalt
Pecking at a grease spot
That was once a rabbit.

Car roars down desert highway—
172 miles from a rodeo
2 hours away.

In the nick of time
Flies low lazy loop.
Lands

On the road again.

Acquired Taste

No matter where roping calves go
They never wipe their feet.
They don't care at all about grooming
Or being tidy and neat.

They stand in trailers full of manure
Souped up by barrels of pee
And mill around in mucky pens
In filth that's ankle deep,

Trot through alleys in more of the same
Then line up in a squalid chute
Stepping in the nasty leavings
Of predecessors who pollute.

Then they do their job in the arena—
Stick three feet up in the air
To be wound up with a piggin' string
That wraps around all that's there.

It stands to reason that piggin' string
Will pick up some residue,
And get coated with slime and corruption
From that dung and urine brew.

So it's absolutely disgusting
And it really grosses me out,
When next time that roper rides in the box
With that piggin' string in his mouth.

Tied for the Average

You're roping ten head, you've got nine on the ground;
The average is calling and you're liking the sound.
You're taking no chances so you load up with ropes
Thinking a second loop will secure all your hopes;
There's a spare pigging string in your belt, just in case,
And a jerk line to put your horse in his place.

You back into the box and nod for your draw,
Play it safe at the barrier to avoid any flaw.
You chase down the calf, which runs straight and true,
And your loop, it has eyes—it knows just what to do.
You reel in the slack and swing out of the saddle
But then trouble arrives—your ropes declare battle.

That second loop, somehow, comes off when you do;
The jerk line gets tangled and unreels all askew.
As you turn and you twist trying to get them undone,
The calf that you caught wants in on the fun.
It circles around you—a lap, maybe two—
Then ducks 'tween your legs and runs right on through.

You're tripped up, tangled up, and flat on your back
Wondering how in the world you got so far off track.
The tie is a legal one—two wraps and a hooey—
Though it's never been done in a way quite this screwy;
But the field judge says—and drops the flag with a laugh—
That the run is a good one and the winner's the calf.

Horses of a Different Color

Among cowboys with
Equine opinions to spare,
You'll often find arguments
About the hair horses wear;

It's one of those topics
That's rife with discord,
Like whether the best
Pickup's a Dodge or a Ford.

They discuss duns and
buckskins, pintos and paints,
Sorrels and chestnuts—
What is, and what ain't.

Some contend white horses
Are really light gray.
And are roans blue and red,
Or can they be bay?

They'll even dispute
When brown turns to black;

And when talk turns to appaloosas,
Well, it never turns back.

They squabble and bicker,
Wrangle and debate,
Histrionically quibble,
Argue and expostulate.

But my opinion's so limited
I don't bother with the brawl;
Name any color you want—
I think I've bucked off 'em all.

So any tone you use or tint you pick
To define a rodeo horse's hue,
There's no arguin' 'bout the rider—
I am, most often, black and blue.

Gear Bag

Contents of gear bag
Idle some 38 years:

1 pretty gold string
    with one remaining tassel, tied to handle.
    (from whiskey bottle)
1 "Enjoy RODEO The All-American Sport"
    badge, pinned to handle.
    (from Justin, since 1879)
2 baggage tags, tattered beyond recognition,
    attached to handle with elastic strings.
    (destination unknown)
1 bareback rigging, with latigos and cinch.
    (Jim Houston body,
    custom rawhide handhold)
1 leather-covered pad.
    (to protect horse's back
    and cowboy's backside)
1 ore sample sack from hard-rock mine, containing:
1 size 8-1/2 leather glove with leather tie strap.
    (stiffened with benzoin
    and coated with rosin)
1 plastic bottle, Rosin, N. F. Lump, 1 pound.
    (Price tag: $2.76, approximately 1/3 full)

1 old plastic rosin bottle, containing:
3 partial rolls of wide adhesive tape;
1 rust-colored sock, knotted, rosin inside.
1 ragged plastic bag
    "COMPLIMENTARY FOR YOUR USE"
    from Stardust, Las Vegas, containing:
1 pair of worn, torn, stitched, riveted, and repaired chaps.
    (white, blue fringe and trim, red stars and belt)
1 pair of boots with split tops and ankle straps.
    (one with tape wrapped around instep, unfamiliar wool socks stuffed inside)
1 pair of custom-made spurs,
    2-1/4 inch offset shanks and flat 5-point star rowels.
1 lifetime's worth of lies and reride stories.
    (partly used)

THREE
Ruminations

Haiku for a Cowboy's Education

I might have been born
naked, but I have since learned
to cover my hide.

Long Time Ago

Tobacco smoke clouded up under his hat brim
    as it drifted slowly from his nose.
He never waved it away, just let it drift and hover,
    crinkling his eye corners closed.

Time was, he said, saddle horses was rank.
    Ever' mornin' they'd rattle
a man from his topknot to his bootheels. But by
    damn, they could work cattle.

In the olden days, he told me, sucking smoke
    from the smoldering butt,
a cowboy had to earn his way to the name.
    Nowadays, any bow-legged strut

With a store-bought shiny buckle holdin' up
    a pair of pants gets called
a cowboy. Hell, kid, the way things is a-goin'
    makes a real hand wanna bawl.

Just before the roll-your-own blistered
    calloused thumb and fingertip
he opened a cut-down Prince Albert can and
    pinched the shreds into the lip.

Damn pen-raised cattle is so soft they
   might as well be pets.
You didn't feed 'em, they'd starve, he said,
   rolling another cigarette.

An orange horn of thumbnail scratched
   flame onto a wood match.
Lungs gasped and wheezed as he sucked heat
   through tobacco thatch.

By damn, we was cowboys, back then,
   me and m' pards, he said.
Ain't no cowboys nowadays, you ask me.
   They're all gone. All dead,

'cept me. Back then.... Aw, what the hell.
   Them days is gone, you know.
Long time ago. Hell, kid, you get to be my age,
   everything's a long time ago.

The Travail, Which God Hath Given

Under the saddle you work,
Dependable and true.
Your purpose reduced to "useful."
You don't feel the jerk
Of the wrangler's loop
Like you did when spirited and youthful—

For you're no hand's pick
As a morning mount
When they're looking to warm their blood
And the work goes quick
And it's speed that counts,
So they call for horses still in the bud.

Oh, there are miles in you yet
And you're nowhere near done;
Still known for being honest and steady;
But you just can't forget
How life once was fun
And for work you were eager and ready.

It was all cut and run
And go fast for that cow
Hell for leather, all out, pushing hard
Till the set of the sun.

But it's brains you use now—
Brawn and muscle replaced with smart.

Faithful through and through,
You do what's expected
For this age is but part of life's plan.
It's what good horses do:
Biding time till rejected
To finish up in a dog food can.

The Second Book of Job

Instead of working horseback and following the cow
I could be afoot behind a horse and following the plow.
Sleeping soft in a cabin, cuddling a baby, loving a wife,
Clear water, and home cooking, a settled kind of life
That's far away, far, far away from the fix I'm in here now.

Here, my belly is my blanket and my back my only bed,
Stone the only pillow on which to lay my bloody head;
Can't even wallow a hip hole where I lie on solid rock.
No one to sing a sad song, no prayers, no soothing talk.
I'm so alone, so all alone, it will be a comfort to be dead.

A stumble on the rimrock; horse and me both took a spill.
He's down, bad hurt and thrashing, beyond my reach to kill
To relieve his pain and misery, so I guess we share our fate
In this lonely place so far away where help will come too late.
And the relief that is my rifle is gone, long gone, downhill.

Death won't be long in coming and I hope I face it brave;
That the pain will treat me gentle so I'll not rant and rave,
Curse the God who made me, or blame Him for this fix.
Let my mind stay clear instead, and resist those devil tricks
And to the end, the very end, thank God for the life He gave.

As clear and as compelling as the clang of a dinner bell
Is the horse's futile scratching at the ground on which he fell,
So the buzzards glide and slide down a drain of azure sky
Studying the menu; watching, waiting, for supper to die.
And only bones, lonely bones, will be left, the story to tell.

Soon my Maker will be asking me if I lived the golden rule
And wonder about my learning in His earthly mortal school.
I'll answer for every wicked thought that ever filled my mind
While hoping they'll be balanced by the times I acted kind
So the tally shows not evil, rather, fool; mere human fool.

Manifest Destiny

Skeletons, like trusses, rafters, beams,
   prop up this trail of ruined dreams
  as parades of hopeful pilgrims tread
a road buttressed by bones of the dead.

Upon Stony Places

Like blood spatter
white stones
cover the field
where babies cried
and buffalo stampeded
and drunkards reeled.

Here, Butler. Bailey,
there. O'Brian,
O'Hara, Horn, Dye.
Jettisoned along Calhoun
Hill, on Battle Ridge, in
Deep Ravine, they lie;

dropped by Runs
The Enemy and Lame
White Man and Rain
In The Face and a
thousand more on
the Greasy Grass. Slain

in a battle fought yet,
bones picked over still,
these honored dead
lie unforgotten
yet unremembered:
Names on stones, unread.

Haiku for Autumn

Frosted barbwire shines
in celestial light, but
the Lord giveth and...

Maple leaves flame out
in cold sun; drift down, down, down
in despair and death.

Blood drips below bowed
branch, antlers scratch epitaph
into deer camp duff.

Fat calves bawl, milk gone
in dustcloud of cows shipped to
where memory dies.

Sleek hides turn shaggy,
worn shoes clank onto rust pile.
Tails hoard cockleburs.

Keeping the Books

It's easier to line out a herd of cattle
    Than sort figures into columns and rows,
But it's not the long hours in the saddle
    That determine if a ranch goes.

It's the nights when you ought to be sleeping,
    Resting up for those cowboying days,
When you ride guard over the bookkeeping
    That determine if a ranch pays.

It's the creak of the leather you live for,
    The pleasure that working horseback gives.
But it's the bills and receipts o'er which you pore
    That determine if a ranch lives.

It's dragging calves to the branding fire,
    It's the roundups you love, and the drives.
But it's the amount on the check from the buyer
    That determines if a ranch survives.

But in the end, when God says it's time to go
    And you finally hang up your tack,
It's all those things that the ledgers don't show
    That tally up to a life in the black.

Semi-Retired

The bail ticks the top wire
and hefted bucket hangs on post.
Hungry horse heads me aside
and noses down into the oats.

My age more than twice over.
He ought to be taking his ease
in the meadow munching clover.
But a kid horse is what he is.

Three times I heave the saddle
before hanging it on his back;
fenders and cinches spraddled
in a hopeless tangle of tack.

Askew blankets, leather awry,
snugged down with a latigo pulled
over crouched shoulder, lifted high
to top out on scuffed-up toes.

Hand over hand up tie strings
boot groping for stirrup hole,
kneeing flank with patched jeans,
snagging horn with an elbow.

He carries me where I want to go
but refuses where danger lurks.
Spent, he turns and trudges home
ignoring rein and quirt.

Calf roping. Western pleasure.
Queen contests. Once won them all.
Silver buckle, trophy spurs,
silk ribbons; faded on tackroom wall.

Hair-side-up blankets cover
saddle tipped on pine pole rail,
steam wisping into autumn air
like the swish of a tired tail.

Bowed neck looped by skinny arm,
headstall pulled over poll and ears;
bit spit from teeth smooth and long.
A kid horse, ending his years.

Haiku for a Horseback Morning

Fetlocks sponge up dew,
waking trail through silver'd green
until the sun climbs.

Gone

With every footfall of the horse, whiskey
sloshes in the bottle in the saddlebag.
The sound of it soothes him. He mops
his face with the bib of his wildrag

and wishes for wind. Biscuit crumbles
in his mouth and he thinks again
of the bottle but instead uncorks the
canteen and splashes the taste of tin

into his mouth and down his throat
and off his chin. On a morning now past
the biscuits had been fresh and water
cool on a tongue flavored with last

night's featherbed ardor. Tonight, he
will wallow a hip hole in the dirt
and tangle with a thin blanket, every
hooch-filled heartbeat diluting the hurt.

Haiku for Hunger

Tomorrow lies in
the curve of a woman's breast
in moonshadow glow.

Packsaddle

For Mother, on her 80th Birthday

No cinches, latigos, or breeching.
No sawbuck tree. No pannier or kyack.
No diamond hitch in a lash rope.
No load stacked or packed on her back.

But when she'd sit, if she'd sit,
between this chore, this job or that,
the bend in the middle made
a lap where, always, something sat:

a bag of groceries back from town,
a book to read, an afghan to crochet,
dresses to hem, shirts to mend,
potatoes to peel, homework to okay.

And babies, owned or borrowed.
Her children, then children grand and great;
family, friends, neighbors, strangers
snuggle up soft and safe and warm and wait

while the packsaddle lap rides them
gently, rocks them easily, down the trail
to dreamland. But no nap for the lap;
it moves on, like a mochila packing the mail.

The Beauty of Mountains

Out there, a man's mile-long morning
shadow runs from the sunrise, rolling over
crease and crest and coulee, elongating
a semblance of the horseback drover

erect atop the prairie. Even at noonday,
when he couldn't shade a single blade
of bluestem, the shadow rider blazons his way—
the only vertical entity round about to invade

the plain. Nothing, nothing else within eyeshot
to distract from, to detract from, to interfere with
the high pride of a mounted man on the long trot,
realizing his own reality of the cowboy myth.

But out here, canyons, cliffs, pinnacles, peaks
swallow man and mount whole. Out here, the sunrise is high up the sky so his shy shadow sneaks
out, slinks back, on a rough and rugged run

over slow terrain, never falling far from its source.
Landscape overshadows; reminds a rider of his place.
Out here, mountains render horseman and horse
an insignificant presence; accepted, solely, by grace.

For DW Groethe

ACKNOWLEDGEMENTS

Many, many folks have inspired, informed, instructed, enabled, and encouraged me in my attempts at poesy. They know who they are and I hope they know how much I value them. On a larger scale, there are organizations (and the people associated with them) who have been instrumental: CowboyPoetry.com and The Center for Western and Cowboy Poetry, Western Writers of America, Cowboy Poets of Utah, the League of Utah Writers, and Idaho Writers League.

Appreciation, as well, to the publishers and editors who have inked up my poems, particularly those in this volume that previously appeared in these periodicals: *Western Horseman* ("Heads or Tails," "Not Counting Saddlebags," "Mule Whisperer," "Barrel Roll," "Semi-Retired"), *American Cowboy* ("Second Opinion," "Tied for the Average," "The Second Book of Job"), *Range Magazine* ("Long Time Ago"), *Roundup* ("Upon Stony Places"), *Rope Burns* ("Preliminary Aftermath"), and *Elko Daily Free Press* ("Riding Old Red"); and the anthology *Brushstrokes & Balladeers* ("Migrations," "Spring Works Sonnet").

Finally, many thanks to Duke and Kimberly Pennell and all the other people at Pen-L Publishing who brought this book to life.

About the Author

 Rod Miller is two-time winner of the Western Writers of America Spur Award—for poetry and short fiction—winner of the Westerners International Poetry Award, Academy of Western Artists Award for Best Poetry Book, and the 2012 Writer of the Year award from the League of Utah Writers. His poetry has appeared in numerous periodicals and anthologies, as well as in his collection, *Things a Cowboy Sees and Other Poems*, and a chapbook, *Newe Dreams*. Also to Rod's credit are several essays on the art and craft of poetry, written for CowboyPoetry.com, and he is a frequent presenter at writers' conferences, workshops, and other events.

In addition to poetry, Rod is author of many magazine articles, three nonfiction books, and four novels, most recently *Rawhide Robinson Rides the Range–True Adventures of Bravery and Daring in the Wild West*, every word of which, of course, is true.

Visit online at www.writerRodMiller.com

www.ingramcontent.com/pod-product-compliance
Lightning Source LLC
LaVergne TN
LVHW011427080426
835512LV00005B/310